FATHER'S DAY

Gifts

Anastasia Suen

Rourke
Educational Media

rourkeeducationalmedia.com

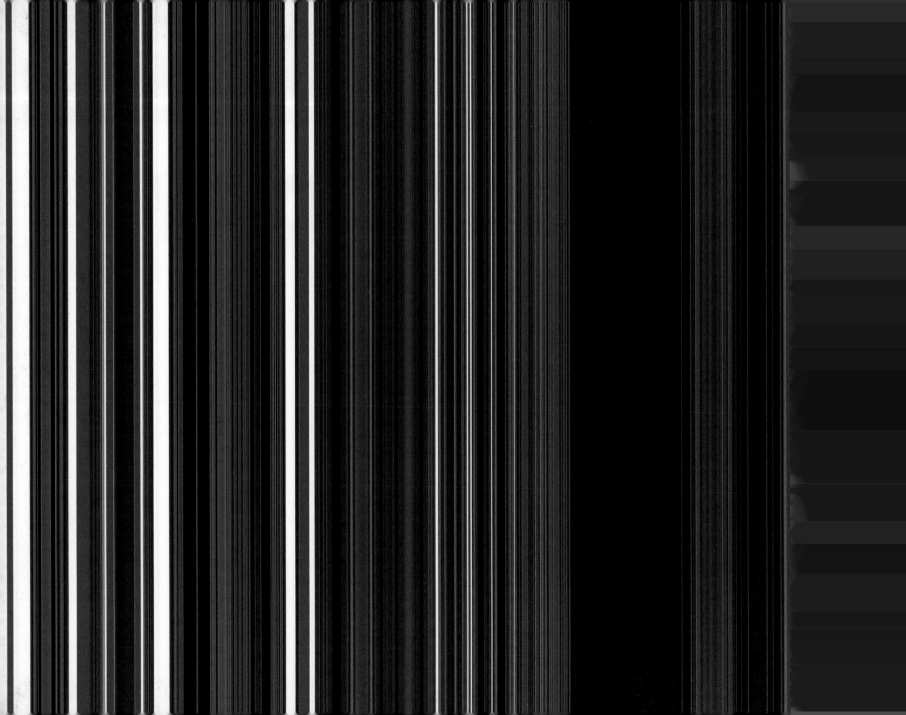

TABLE OF CONTENTS

Materials Needed for All Projects   5

Father's Day Gifts   6

Yarn Block Print   7

Faux Wrought Iron   11

Comic Book Coasters   15

Golden Hand   19

Hero Plaque   23

Sports Fleece Blanket   27

Glossary   30

Index   31

Show What You Know   31

Websites to Visit   31

About the Author   32

MATERIALS NEEDED FOR ALL PROJECTS

- acrylic spray
- air dry clay
- black spray paint
- bowl
- ceramic tiles
- ceramic tiles
- clear acrylic spray (optional)
- felt
- fleece
- glue or **decoupage**
- masking tape
- measuring tape or ruler
- metal nuts, bolts, and gears
- newspaper or cloth to cover your work area
- paint
- paintbrush or foam brush
- paper
- paper rolls (from toilet paper and paper towels)
- pencil or pen
- picture frame
- plastic knife
- plastic mat or wax paper
- rolling pin
- scissors
- small bowl
- small wooden block
- unfinished wood plaque
- yarn
- wood letters
- wood stain

FATHER'S DAY GIFTS

Celebrate Father's Day by making a special gift. Create art with yarn, paint, wood, and paper. Cut and tie a no-sew sports fleece blanket. **Sculpt** a golden hand. Make a hero plaque and superhero coasters for the superhero in your life—your dad!

TIP!

Make Father's Day extra special this year with these unique gifts.

You Will Need:
- newspaper or cloth to cover your work area
- yarn
- scissors
- small wooden block
- paint (your father's favorite color)
- paintbrush
- large sheet of art paper
- extra sheet of paper for practice
- pencil or pen
- picture frame

Make art with yarn, paint, and a block of wood.

Here's How:

1. Wrap yarn around a small wooden block.
2. Cut the end of the yarn. Tie a knot.

TIP!

As you wrap the yarn around the block, leave some spaces open. Wrap at a **diagonal** in some places to make an X or a V pattern.

3. Turn the block over. Paint the yarn.
4. Press the painted yarn on the paper.
5. Turn the corner of the block. Make a new print next to the first one.
6. Repeat until you reach the end. Then start a new line and keep going.
7. Add more paint to the block as needed.

8. After you print the entire sheet, let the paint dry.

9. Sign your name. Add the date. Then frame your gift.

Negative Space Grid

For a different effect, add more **negative** space around each block as you print. Leave an empty border around the **grid** and only print the middle of the paper.

TIP!

The space around the lines in your painted grid is called negative space. Negative space helps viewers see the shapes you have created.

TIP!

Faux (pronounced FOH) is a French word that means false or fake.

Make a faux wrought iron sculpture with paper rolls.

TIP!

Wrought iron often has a **symmetrical** pattern. The design on one side matches the design on the other side.

Here's How:

1. Remove the glass, paper, and cardboard from the picture frame.
2. Place drawing paper under the empty frame and make sketches.
3. Cut each paper roll open.

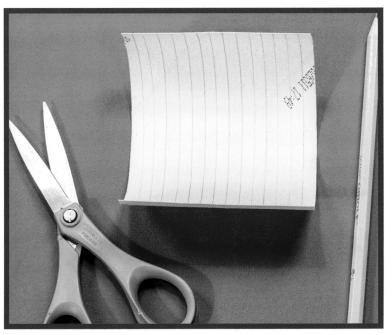

4. Use a ruler and mark each quarter inch (6 millimeters).
5. Draw a line at each mark.
6. Cut the paper into thin strips.

TIP!

Cut the long paper towel rolls into long strips. You can use the long strips to divide the frame into sections.

13

7. Fold or curl the paper to make shapes.
8. Place the shapes inside the frame.
9. Glue each shape in place.
10. After the glue dries, take the frame outside.
11. Spray the paper and the frame black. Ask an adult to help you.

14

Make four superhero comic book coasters for the superhero in your life—your dad!

Here's How:

1. Measure the ceramic tiles.
2. Find comics large enough to cover each tile.

You Will Need:

- newspaper or cloth to cover your work area
- comic book pages
- scissors
- pencil
- 4 ceramic tiles with rounded edges
- decoupage
- paintbrush or foam brush
- felt
- glue
- clear acrylic spray (optional)

TIP!
You can use old comics or make color copies of comics you find online. Let the ink dry before you cut the pages.

3. Place the tile over the comic. Draw a line around the edges.
4. Cut the comic to match the tile size.

7. Spread decoupage on top of each tile.
8. Place a comic face up on each tile.
9. Gently smooth out any air bubbles.
10. Cover the comic with decoupage.
11. Let the tiles dry overnight.

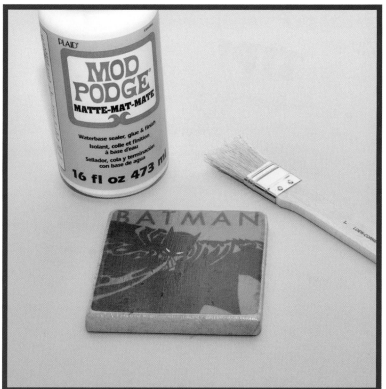

12. Cover the top with decoupage two more times. Let the tiles dry each time. The decoupage will go on white, but it will dry clear. If you use **glossy** decoupage, it will also be shiny when it dries.

13. Glue felt squares to the back.

14. Wrap your gift in Sunday comics.

TIP!

To waterproof the tiles, ask an adult to spray them with clear acrylic spray after the final coat of decoupage dries.

Golden Hand

Here's How:

1. Warm up the clay with your hands. Then roll it on a clean surface.

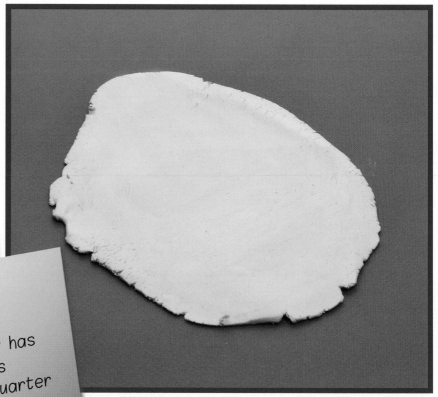

You Will Need:
- plastic mat or wax paper to cover your work area
- air dry clay
- rolling pin
- pencil
- plastic knife
- small bowl
- paintbrush
- gold paint

TIP!

Use a rolling pin to make sure the clay has the same thickness throughout. One-quarter inch (6 millimeters) is best.

2. Place your hand on the clay. Keep your fingers close together.

3. Draw a line around your fingers. Press the pencil all the way down.

4. After you lift your hand, draw a half circle at the bottom.

5. Use the pencil to draw **shallow** lines between the fingers.

6. Cut away the clay around your handprint.

7. Place the clay hand inside a small bowl to dry.

TIP!

Let the clay hand dry palm up for a few hours. Then turn the hand and the bowl over to dry the back.

When you remove the dry hand from the bowl, it will look curved like this.

8. After the clay is dry, paint it gold on both sides.

Not a fan of gold? You can paint your hand any color you like!

Add Patterns:

Before you dry the clay, you can add a pattern to the hand. Press the bottom of a pencil into the clay to make a small circle. Use toothpicks or a fork to make rows of dotted lines. You can even draw fingernails with a pencil. Just be careful not to press the pencil all the way through.

Make a hero plaque for your dad.

Here's How:

1. Brush wood stain on the plaque.
2. Let the stain dry.

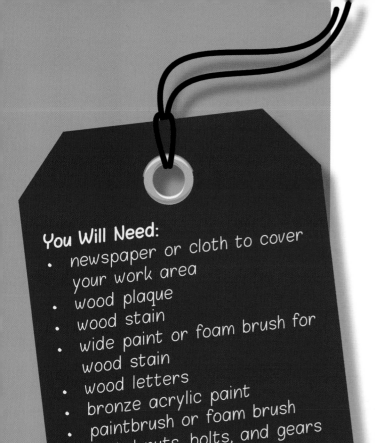

You Will Need:

- newspaper or cloth to cover your work area
- wood plaque
- wood stain
- wide paint or foam brush for wood stain
- wood letters
- bronze acrylic paint
- paintbrush or foam brush
- metal nuts, bolts, and gears
- glue

TIP!

You can find unfinished wood plaques in different shapes and sizes at many craft supply stores.

3. Paint the letters bronze.

4. Let the bronze paint dry.

5. Glue the letters to the plaque.

6. Glue on metal nuts, bolts, and gears.

TIP!

Place the letters and nuts and bolts in a design you like before you glue them.

Tack It On

Have a longer message? Type it in color on the computer and print it on thick paper. Fasten the message to the plaque with furniture tacks. Hammer a tack into each corner of the paper.

DAD

Thanks For Being My Hero!

Make your father a sports blanket.

Here's How:

1. Clean up the edge of the fleece. Cut off the **selvedge**.
2. Trim the other edges as needed to make them straight.

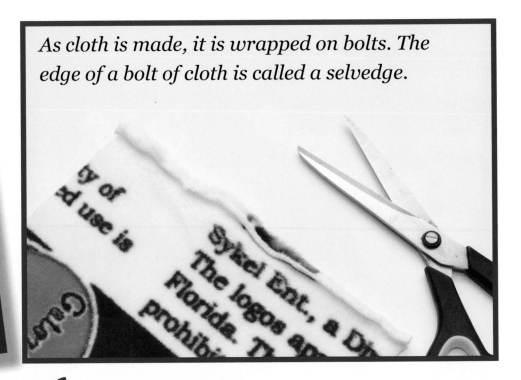

As cloth is made, it is wrapped on bolts. The edge of a bolt of cloth is called a selvedge.

DID YOU KNOW?

Fleece comes in both 48 inch (122 centimeter) and 60 inch (152 centimeter) widths. Ask the store clerk to cut the fabric so you can make a 48 inch by 60 inch (122 centimeter by 152 centimeter) blanket.

3. Place masking tape four inches (10 centimeters) from the edge.
4. Cut out the square in each corner.
5. Place the measuring tape above the masking tape. Mark the tape at each inch (2.54 centimeters).
6. Cut from the edge of the cloth to the marks on the tape.

7. Cut fringe on all four sides of the blanket.
8. Remove the masking tape. Tie a knot at the top of each strand of fringe.

TIP!

If you want to make a thicker blanket, you can use two layers of fleece.

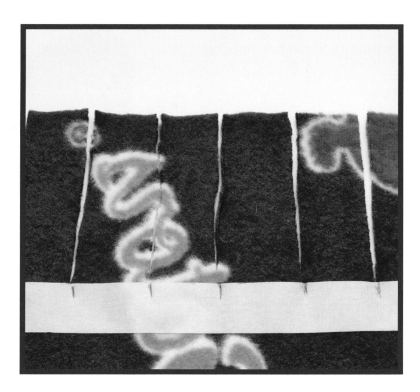

GLOSSARY

decoupage (day-koo-PAHZH): glue used to hold and seal paper to another item

diagonal (dye-AG-uh-nuhl): a straight line between opposite corners

faux (FOH): false or fake

glossy (GLAWSS-ee): with a shiny surface

grid (grid): evenly spaced lines that form squares

negative (NEG-uh-tiv): the absence of something

sculpt (SKUHLPT): to make a model of something

selvedge (SEL-vij): the edge of a bolt of cloth

shallow (SHAL-oh): not deep

symmetrical (si-MET-ruh-kuhl): matching on both sides

wrought (RAWT): shaped by beating it with a hammer

INDEX

blanket 6, 27, 28, 29

clay 20, 21, 22

coasters 6, 15, 16

decoupage 16, 17, 18

iron 11, 12

paint 6, 8, 9, 10, 12, 20, 22, 24, 25

paper 6, 8, 9, 10, 12, 13, 14, 26

plaque 6, 23, 24, 25, 26

wood 6, 8, 24

yarn 6, 7, 8, 9

SHOW WHAT YOU KNOW

1. How did you make a grid with the painted yarn block?

2. Why do works of art have negative space?

3. How do you make the comic book coasters waterproof?

4. Describe the steps used to make the clay hand form a curved shape.

5. Why do you need a measuring tape or a ruler to make a blanket?

WEBSITES TO VISIT

www.ourfamilyworld.com/2012/05/18/fathers-day-crafts-for-kids/

www.happyfamilyart.com/art-lessons/mixed-media-art-lessons/air-dry-clay-art-projects-or-adventures-with-clay/

www.artistshelpingchildren.org/kidscraftsactivitiesblog/2011/11/how-to-make-a-no-sew-water-bottle-holder/

ABOUT THE AUTHOR

As a child, Anastasia Suen made and wrapped Father's Day gifts at the kitchen table. Today she uses that same kitchen table to make and wrap Father's Day gifts in her studio in Northern California.

Meet The Author!
www.meetREMauthors.com

www.rourkeeducationalmedia.com

PHOTO CREDITS: All photos © Blue Door Publishing, FL except the following from Shutterstock.com: page 2-3 © Vladeep; page 6 © 7th Sun; post-it notes throughout © InshStyle; page 7 © Roman King; page 26 plaque (without the saying) © Flas100; page 30 © Patty Chan

Edited by: Keli Sipperley

Cover and Interior design by: Nicola Stratford   www.nicolastratford.com
Thank you, Ashley Hayasaka, for making the crafts.

Library of Congress PCN Data

Father's Day Gifts / Anastasia Suen
 (Craft It!)
  ISBN 978-1-68342-372-0 (hard cover)
  ISBN 978-1-68342-881-7 (soft cover)
  ISBN 978-1-68342-538-0 (e-Book)
Library of Congress Control Number: 2017931272

Rourke Educational Media
Printed in the United States of America, North Mankato, Minnesota